THE BENCH

by Darla Dodds

DORRANCE PUBLISHING CO
EST. 1920
PITTSBURGH, PENNSYLVANIA 15238

Dorrance Publishing Co
585 Alpha Drive
Pittsburgh, PA 15238
Visit our website at *www.dorrancebookstore.com*

ISBN: 979-8-8892-5392-1
eISBN: 979-8-8892-5892-6

THE
BENCH

Acknowledgments

This book is dedicated to my Dad, who's life of character, strength, wisdom and compassion has challenged me to catch life's lessons from every day experiences, and inspired me to use the power of the pause.

I would like to say thank you to:
The champion of my home and the love of my life, my husband Rusty Dodds, who lifts me up on wings like an eagle to expand my vision, help me see the bigger picture and reach further for my dreams than I ever thought possible.
My biggest encouragers: my sister, my Mom and my closest friends.
My Lord and Savior Jesus Christ

Finally, to you, the Reader. Thank you for picking up this book. I hope you can insert your own story and life-lessons into this book. I hope that you will be able to remember and celebrate the good things that you experienced; and take the lessons learned along the journey to help you through whatever you are going through right now. Maybe this book will also remind you that you have lessons and gifts to pass on to others you encounter. Give generously, you never know who's life you will change for the good.

Scripture quotations are from the New King James Version of the Bible.

Introduction

Desperate to clear my mind today, I just started driving. I had a million places I had to be today and just as many things to do, but at this moment, I made a decision to drive, with no specific destination in mind and no idea what I would do when I reached this unknown place. I was seeking relief from the rushing river of emotions in my head. I was seeking wisdom to make choices and take needed action. I was looking for strength and renewal. Maybe I was even just running away. With all that flooding my mind, I set out and started driving and driving. I was hours from anyplace familiar to me, but the drive was doing me good.

Finally I came across a beautiful lake with a hiking trail around it. I thought to myself, *Ah, this will be a perfect place to enjoy the beauty of fall. I can pray, be present in the moment, and get my thoughts together.* The cool breeze gave me a chill while the sun streamed down, hugging me with its warmth. The smell of fall was in the air, and taking a deep breath, I smiled because this is my favorite season. The dry leaves crunched under my feet as I walked. My eyes scanned the beauty of nature. Rays of sun cut through the vibrant yellow, red, orange, and green masterpiece of colors donning the tree canopies. Squirrels scurried through the branches playfully while birds flew and lit in nearby trees. This place was so peaceful, so tranquil, so amazingly gorgeous! My thoughts stopped racing as I became fully engulfed in the beauty all around me.

As I walked and became engrossed in my surroundings, that was when I noticed something peculiar. There it was, a short distance off the main trail, discolored, weathered, and worn. The fall leaves were lying untouched on its wood surface. It looked like something once used a long time ago but now forgotten. Trees and brush have grown up over the years, blocking what looked like a beautiful view of the lake. I wonder about the craftsman of this bench and the stories and talks that might have been overheard when this bench was used. I wonder who sat on this bench and if their stories still live on.

Suddenly the heavy load of worries I was carrying earlier in the day was replaced with vivid pictures in my imagination of people who have come and gone through time and have gotten to enjoy this bench. I noticed a smile on my face and felt a little lighter in my step as the creative images kept pouring in and I walked into this new adventure.

Chapter 1

The owner of this beautiful piece of land walked for a long time, looking for the perfect spot to build the bench. He finally found the right location. He had such an eye for beauty and wanted to showcase the lake and the splendor of the surrounding hills. The trees and brush were carefully trimmed to reveal the best and most stunning view of the lake, which glistened like diamonds in the afternoon sun. The Craftsman built the bench sturdy and used solid oak and the best of all materials. It was carefully designed to last many years, bringing blessings to the countless people who came to enjoy the lake. The smell of the new wood tickled his nose as he smiled proudly at his craftsmanship. He inscribed an inspirational message. He was pleased with his work and sat on the bench, imagining all that was to come.

It had to be a fall day, much like today when the young lady, thirty-nine weeks into her pregnancy, came upon this bench and sat down slightly out of breath. It had been getting harder to walk during this past week because the baby had dropped down significantly, and it looked like he was going to be right on time for his projected day of his birth. While she sat on the bench and scanned the lake and the beautiful scene, the baby gave a sharp kick in her belly.

The young lady rubbed her belly and spoke softly to her unborn child, "Just a few more days, little one, I can tell you are eager to start your adventure." She wondered about her son and what it would be like to have a second child. The first one was now two-years-old, and it was so exciting for her to have children, especially boys. She was filled with **hope and expectation**. As she pondered, she remembered some beautiful words she had heard before, *"I knitted you together in your mother's womb, you are fearfully and wonderfully made."*

The wiggly little boy was three-years-old. He was on the bench with his mom. He couldn't sit still and was so excited to be watching his dad work under the hood of the shiny red Mac truck. He strained for a better view and longed to see the big engine inside the truck. The boy was so curious, so interested in what his dad was doing. His mom noticed his interest and smiled at him. He carried such **excitement and anticipation** when he was learning something new. Then the little boy's attention was drawn to the toy truck in his own hand, and he began taking the wheels off the truck as he tried to understand what makes them spin.

Even as he grew, the young boy remained curious about how things worked. He took everything apart. If it had screws, he unscrewed it. He once took his mom's vacuum sweeper apart, and she discovered it in pieces when she went to sweep the floor. His mom marveled at his **curiosity and desire to learn**. Would he grow up to be an inventor or engineer some day? The little boy's dad continued to teach him to use various tools as they worked together on that Mac truck. There were times when the young boy sat down on the bench, exhausted after washing and waxing his dad's truck. He quickly learned to **do it right the first time**, or his dad would have him do it again until it was correct. He was becoming **strong and independent.**

As I walked the trail by the lake and imagined the lives and activities of the unknown people who came to the bench, the stories began to get more vivid as they became a combination of some true things in my life and some things that were simply imagination. I did not realize until now that my mind must have been on my dad. Maybe I was wishing he was there with me that day to help me through my struggles and worry of the day. Maybe my subconscious mind was wrestling with how to let my dad know his impact on my life. Maybe somehow, as I was feeling so alone today, that I was dreading the day my dad is no longer with me on this earth when he can't help me solve the problems of my life or provide me with insight beyond my own understanding…I don't know and I didn't have much time to ponder that further because the stories of the bench continued to manifest in my mind. I could see and hear them so vividly, it was almost like watching the scenes of a movie begin to unfold.

I heard the sounds first, which made me look in their direction. There were some young teens sitting on the bench, laughing, listening to music, and just having fun. My mind wondered to what my dad was like in his teen years… I've always envisioned him as a tough guy driving fast muscle cars, the kind of guy no one dared to mess with. His nickname was "Punk," and I have always imagined that he was a bit of a rebel with a sparkle in his eyes, always up for the next challenge. I also believed that he was the kind of guy that if someone told him that he can't do or have something that he would find a way to do it in spite of them. Strong willed? Or strong leader? His siblings are too eager to share stories about things my dad did, but they also tell on themselves when they share. That reminds me of a story I heard about my dad. When he was in high school, he kept passing the school bus. He was warned that if he did it one more time, he would not graduate. Well guess what …

The young man was eighteen-years old and sat heavily on the bench. His arms were crossed, his face was hot with anger. His mind replayed the argument with his father from earlier that day, just infuriating him even more. He thought about how unfair his father had been and that it would not have been difficult at all for his father to help him out. He wanted that car more than anything. He had gone by the showroom hundreds of times. He visualized himself driving it. He couldn't wait! That shiny new car was going to be all his! Now was the time for him to get that car, but his dad wouldn't even help him! He knew about hard work and he knew he could pay his father back, but his father was having nothing of it. Still stewing in anger, the young man looked at the scene in front of him as if he was scanning the whole world wondering what to do with his life. Before he knew it, he was signed up to go into the Army.

"That will show him …" Little did he know, he was learning a lesson from his father about **saving money, instant gratification, planning for the future, and being cautious about taking out loans with compounding interest working against him.** Later he would use that lesson he learned to **pay off a thirty-year mortgage in fifteen years by doubling the payments.**

Chapter 2

The Craftsman of the bench looked on and smiled as he saw young couples enjoying the bench and the children running around the bench as their parents talked. He watched with joy when people used the bench to pray, or read, or just relax in the summer sun. The bench was sturdy and strong and represented so much that is good in life, like strength and health, family, faith, adventures, memories, and rest. The Craftsman inscribed a message on the bench for the people.

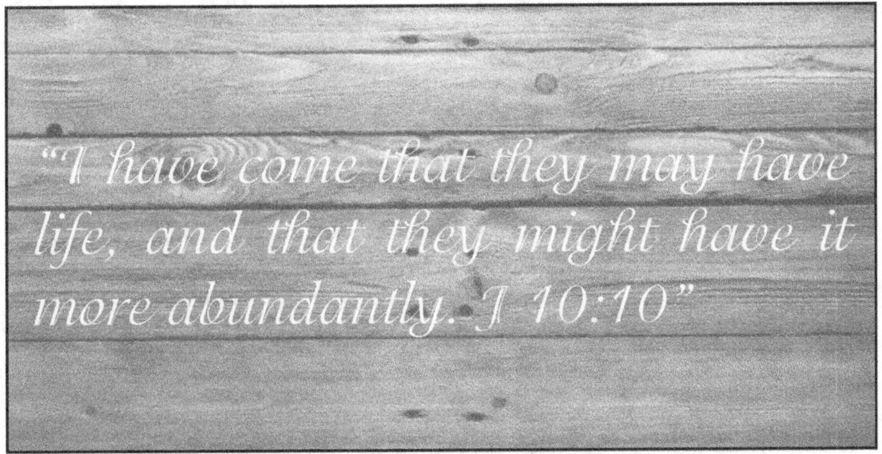

As I watched the young couple sitting on the bench together, holding hands and looking out over the beautiful water and scenic view, the man leaned over and gently kissed the lady on the cheek. This was one of their favorite places to come, and they just felt such peace and freedom here. They talked and talked about everything and enjoyed being so connected and open. Their love and understanding of each other only grew stronger when they came to this special place. I wondered what it was like when my mom and dad met each other…Did he go regularly to the car hop because the food was great or was it because of that young waitress who always seemed to be working when he arrived at the restaurant? Was he shy or bold when he talked to her? Did she blush when she noticed his gaze in her direction? Did they look for each other in town when they cruised around in their cars? When he took her out on a date, did they sit on the bench and watch the beautiful sunset over the lake?

At some point, after dating and spending time together, the young couple decided to get married. In fact they had been waiting until the young waitress turned twenty-one, so she could consent to her own marriage, then three days later, they were married. The expectations, "work hard, get married, and have children," which were taught mostly by example by their family, were ringing in their ears. They had so much in common as they were both hard workers, fiercely independent, enjoyed the same things, and they were ready for the adventure of marriage and a family. One day after they were married, when they were sitting on the bench talking about their future dreams, they talked about having children. They decided that if they were going to have children, they would make an agreement to **teach their children something new every day.**

I was having so much fun as I walked on the hiking trails around the lake. I had no idea how long I had been there, and I was so caught up in the stories of the bench that I also didn't know how far I had walked. I guess it really didn't matter. All the many places I had to go and all the things on my list to do were not even near as important as what I was experiencing at the lake. My dad has talked often of his plan with my mom to teach us girls one new thing every day. As the stories of the bench started to unfold, it was evident that the stories showed examples of the many lessons that were taught and caught as my parents maneuvered the journey of raising children.

Then the children came, first a daughter, then thirteen months later, a second daughter (that was me!). Of course for me, these early years are not something I remember directly, but I can see from the home movies how much fun and enjoyment my parents had with us girls. I could also see even in the movies how they were fulfilling their promise to each other, to teach their children at least one new thing every day. Infants grow to toddlers and toddlers to children, and it all happens so quickly, with milestone after milestone of new experiences and new skills being developed.

Some of those early lessons involved the way I saw my parents interact with other people. I learned things like **"be kind to strangers"** as my dad picked up hitchhikers and gave them a ride. My sister and I would often be sandwiched between my dad and the stranger on the bench seat in our pickup truck. I learned to **"give a little of what I have"** as I watched my dad invest in the life of a homeless man who came by our house often and joined us for dinner and had some conversation with my dad. We saw this guy a lot, and I watched him really transform his life as he spent time with my dad. I'm sure there were lessons involving **"don't judge others"** when we first met this homeless man in his disheveled and unkempt state.

Quickly we learned to **"clean up after ourselves"** by taking our dishes to the sink. When we went camping, we would learn to **"leave the place better than we found it,"** as my parents would have us walk all around the campsite, picking up trash before we left. It's funny, for some lessons, it took us more time and frustrations before we learned the lesson that **"it's better just to do the thing than to argue about doing it or put it off."** My sister and I argued with each other over who was going to wash and who was going to dry the dishes for what seemed like hours, and when we were finally done, we still had the sink full of dishes waiting for us. It would have been nice to learn that lesson a bit earlier.

Not only did my dad expect that my sister and I would learn something new every day, but he, too, is a hungry student and continuous learner. I've watched him read and study for hours various things of interest to him, like wild game hunting, looking at maps and linking them to historical towns and landmarks, treasure hunting, inventing and building things, running, and working on computers. I learned to have a **passion for learning**, to **ask questions and be curious**. I found that if I wanted to get good at something, not only do I need to practice, but I need to **learn what others who have gone before me have done, especially the experts.**

Some of those memories and lessons learned came back so vividly that it was almost like I was experiencing them again!

I noticed the man who sat on the bench after his morning run. My mind was immediately taken back to that time when that man was my dad. The sweat was pouring off of him, and his breathing and heart rate were still elevated. His lungs were screaming at him, and he coughed violently after years of smoking.

As uncomfortable as it was, he was committed to continue the life of a non-smoker and to get healthy. It really wasn't the desire to get healthy that moved him in this direction, nor was it the "lessons" his daughters taught him after a smoking cessation program at school. Really it was just a dad's desire to keep his daughter safe. That daughter is me. I was eight-years-old and I was in the downtown park after local runners had run a 10K race. I saw the table with all the shiny trophies. I came home that evening and told my dad that I wanted to run the race next year, so I could win the big trophy. My dad knew I had to train, and in order to run that distance, it would mean running on the road, and he did not want me to run alone. He quit smoking and started to run with me.

As I watched my dad quit smoking, push through the pain in his lungs caused from a lifetime of smoking, and actually getting good at running, I learned a lesson that would show up many times in my life, **"you can do anything if you put your mind to it and push through."** There were so many great talks, laughs, challenges, heartbreaks, and victories and great lessons as we ran together. These lessons in my early years were some of the most powerful ones that helped shape me in my life. I learned lessons, such as **don't quit, finish strong, endurance (keep going), set goals, and strive for your personal best and you can do more than you think you can.** One day my dad and I were out for some long slow distance, and as we ran and talked, I noticed we got further and further from the house. At times I tried to dig in my heels and refuse to go further, but we both felt good, so we kept running. We ended up running twenty-four miles that day! If you were to ask me to run twenty-four miles at that time, I would have probably told you I could not. Maybe my dad knew that was a limiting belief of mine, so he tricked me into hitting that goal, into doing more than I thought I could do. I also learned about **the power words like "tempo" and of visualization.** To actually "see" yourself going through the race with a smooth, steady pace, light as a feather, strong and steady breathing, feeling great, feeling strong, and crossing that finish line after giving it your best. Running with my dad also taught me **how to deal with the heartache and disappointment** of not winning and how to be a good sport. Oh, but I really like to win and I can be very competitive. There were many more victories than disappointments and stacks of trophies and medals won by both my dad and me over those years.

There are certain sounds and smells that take me right back to some of the fondest memories of growing up and spending time with my dad.

I heard the sound of a chainsaw running in the nearby woods. As I looked around, I noticed that my dad was not at the house. I got my sister, and she and I ran through the leaf-covered trails in the woods, following the sound of the running chainsaw until we could see our dad in the distance. We learned that he could not hear us we approached when the chainsaw was running, so we kept our distance, **being aware of our environment** and looking for which direction the tree would fall. When the tree fell and he shut off the chainsaw, my sister and I ran in to greet him. I don't know what it was that I liked so much about this scene and cutting firewood. It certainly was not the stacking of the fire wood that I enjoyed! That job was tiresome because so often we did not stack it correctly and had to stack it again. I know now my dad was just trying to keep us safe so that the wood pile did not fall on us, but it sure was exhausting work! So we quickly learned the lesson my dad learned so early in his own life, **do it right the first time**.

Whatever it was that brought such excitement back then, when I hear the sound of a chainsaw, or when I smell the smell of the freshly cut wood, or see the sawdust litter the ground, it still creates that same hopeful, excited reaction in me today! I suppose it was probably just **time with Dad**, knowing he was pleased with us, the **fulfillment of doing hard work** and **finishing the job**, that sense of satisfaction. Many of the lessons of the daily chores helped us learn to **jump in and help when needed and don't wait to be asked to help.** Of course I loved the reaping the benefits of all that hard work when we were able to burn wood in our fireplace during the winter. The soft glow, the heat, the family times around the fire.

My dad is not a hugely sentimental guy, so you can imagine how challenging it must have been having two very sensitive and emotional daughters. I'm sure we did all kinds of things in an attempt to make him proud of us, to notice us.

We often said, "Look at me daddy!" or "Watch this!" Caught up in our own little worlds or in our own insecurities, we kept seeking that validation, and I know as an adult that he always noticed, he was always watching, and that he was and is proud of us.

My sister and I probably had everything that a child could need or want. A mom and dad who loved us, a beautiful house in the country with plenty of woods in which to play, safe and friendly neighbors, a club house, go carts, mini bikes, and even a tee pee and totem pole! We had a sled riding hill that was the envy of the neighbors, and my dad even strung lights on it so we could sled ride in the evening! Since my sister and I were so close in age, we did a lot of things together, but my parents made sure that they did special things with each of us, and we learned about **fair, not equal**. They helped us learn about **making decisions** by gathering information from different sources, then thinking it through to make a decision. **We learned about choice,** and of course lessons in choice usually have **lessons in consequences,** good or bad. My parents were very innovative and therefore challenged us to **find creative solutions** to our projects at school and to **go above and beyond** the minimum requirements. We learned that **it was ok to try and fail, then learn from the experience and try again.**

We had some opportunities to learn some early **entrepreneurial and business skills** by picking and selling berries and having yard sales. Later I learned to watch for end of season clearance sales for big ticket items, like prom gowns, which I discovered I could purchase brand new for 75 percent off, then hold them over the winter and re-sell them during prom season. I guess I was learning to **look for opportunities.**

My dad is a treasure hunter and history enthusiast, so he often studied stories about the old oil towns or battles from the Revolutionary War or the

French and Indian War. He would study the stories, books, and articles he was reading about these historic places, looking for hints on the locations. Then he would study maps to find them. If the locations were on public lands, he would then set out to go treasure hunting either for old bottles or with his metal detector, looking for old coins and artifacts. He taught me **how to spot signs** that a town used to be in an area from the rock foundations to a strange patch of daffodils growing in the middle of the woods. I believe my dad could see the stories of the people in these towns or battlefields. He could see children climbing trees or playing in the yard. He could see soldiers camped out resting before the next battle. If he found a piece of jewelry, usually a ring, he would think about the person who wore it and what they might have been doing when they lost it. My dad helped me **learn to solve problems logically** and how to enjoy the thrill of it all coming together after the hard work.

It took an amazing amount of skill in map reading, including topographical maps and knowledge of history and how towns built up around railroads and rivers. It's no wonder that not only did I believe my dad was the strongest man in the world, but I also believed he was the smartest man in the world! I have not really understood the value of studying history, except in seeing it through his eyes and in the cool treasures he dug up and brought home. I really enjoyed looking at what he found and even helping to clean them up and then to do more research and find that "piece," for example a brass eagle head that would have been used as a saddle horn and find it connected to the battle in a book. Then the history really came alive. I did not understand the value of the study of history until much later, probably into my adult life.

Of course there were the **character/integrity** lessons, such as **treat others as you would like to be treated, do not take the Lord's name in vain, do not gossip,** and **silence is consent.** It took me awhile before I understood what my dad meant by "silence is consent." It showed up when other kids at school picked on someone or bullied them. My dad let me know that I was just as guilty as those being mean to someone if I just stood by and did not say anything. It was like I agreed with their actions. In another context, when people get in a group and talk badly about another person or gossip about them and I say nothing, my silence means I agree with them. This was a tough lesson because none of us want the rath of a bully focused in our direction, but with some **courage,** it was a great **lesson on humanity and valuing people.**

There were also lessons about **owning your mistakes and not telling lies.** One day our pet cat jumped up onto the counter and got into the butter. My parents asked us about this, and we protected the cat by telling a lie that we used a fork in the butter. My dad told us he would write down in his black book this lie that we told and that he would also write down any other lies that we told in the future. I don't think he ever said what would happen if we told lies and they got written in the book, but our imagination of what *could* happen was certainly enough to deter us. From that day forward, my sister and I were terrified to tell a lie.

Anyone who knows my dad would say that something very important to him is **if you say you are going to do something, do it.** My dad is true to his word, and I could always and can still expect that if my dad says he will do something, he will do it. I can count on him, and he has never been wishy-washy. This, too, is an integral part of me, and I have found myself doing whatever it takes to fulfill my word to someone if I told them I would do something.

Chapter 3

Season after season have passed, and the bench stood strong. It stood up to the mighty storms and the hot scorching sun. At times it was soaked by rain or frozen in the snow. The Craftsman worked carefully on the bench to patch and reinforce it. The Craftsman was glad that he had made it so strong in the beginning because the bench had touched so many lives throughout the years. He saw so many people who leaned on the bench or sat down exhausted after life had hit them hard, then he saw them gain their strength, renew their thoughts, and begin to dream again or to set out to tackle the next obstacle. The Craftsman inscribed a message on the bench to encourage the people when they were tired and help them find their strength again. Oh, how he loved the people.

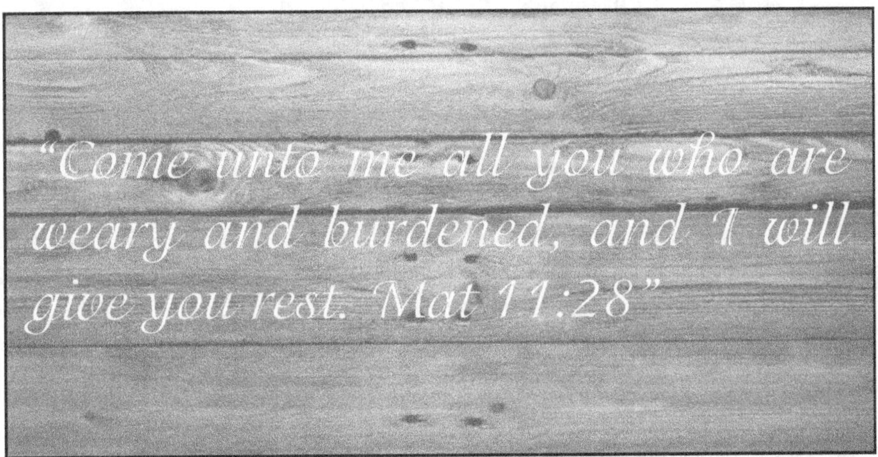

It is likely as I share this part of the story that the information might be distorted from what really happened, but here it is through the eyes and perspective of a young girl. My parents did not fight, at least not in front of my sister or me, but there came to be a strange silence in our home. It felt cold and made my sister and me uneasy, but we did not understand. Sometimes we tip-toed out to the landing of the staircase where we could look out over the living room. From that vantage point, we looked on when things seemed tense between my parents.

It has been said that the very thing that attracted people to each other can be the very thing that breaks them apart. My mom worked a lot and spent long hours at the restaurant. It was common that we would go to the diner to visit her while she worked. I really enjoyed our trips to the diner to see my mom! I learned how to choose a lighter dinner, so that I could enjoy a dessert or a cold milkshake. Those milkshakes that you only get in a diner. They serve the milkshake in a glass, plus you get the stainless-steel cup with the extra milkshake in it to refill your glass! We'd visit with Mom for a while when we ate, and sometimes we got to hang out with her after we were done eating and we could help out in the kitchen or cleaning up the tables.

We saw both of our parents working hard and working a lot. We adjusted our play and being noisy sometimes when my dad worked the third shift and had to sleep during the day. Well we attempted to. I'm quite certain we woke Dad up all the time with our giggles, or running around the house, or talking on the phone. The phone was connected with a cord to a wall at that time, and the phone was right outside my parents' bedroom.

Since both of my parents worked, it would be common for my sister and I to get ourselves up for school and also to return from school before my parents got home from work. They must have taught us well because we both did everything we could not to miss the bus in the morning, even if that meant running up the road or riding our bicycle to school. Maybe we did not want to make hardship for our parents, but probably it was because we did not want to get in trouble or disappoint them. In fact that lead to us having perfect attendance most school years and good grades. I guess a few of the lessons at that time include: **Get where you are supposed to go by whatever means necessary**, and **consistent action in the right direction can lead to success.**

I don't know when things got bad enough for my mom and dad to separate. I don't know how those discussions went. I don't know either side of their stories. I do know that there was a day that my mom moved out. I remember having a deep hurt and being angry with her (an anger I held for many years) and I remember suddenly feeling unsafe and unloved for possibly the first time in my life. I watched my family shatter right in front of my eyes, and before I knew it, my dad was single and raising two daughters. Through this story, I am not villainizing my mom, in fact I love her very much. It just happened to be at the time the decisions were made, that it was more logical for my sister and me to live with my dad, and therefore that is the course my story took.

There were so many lessons caught during this time. I watched my dad **keep on keeping on, even when things were tough.** I watched my dad **get back up when he got knocked down.** I don't remember him ever saying mean things about my mom to my sister or me. The earlier lessons stood firm, **do not gossip.** My dad had to keep finding ways to solve problems (most of which I am unaware of) because he let my sister and I be kids. We were aware of but not caught up in the struggles of the most significant adults in our lives. There just was not a lot of talking about it.

Although we had experienced loss of beloved pets or distant relatives, the intensity of the pain that this divorce brought on was probably the **first major loss** in our lives. Somehow, despite how we felt, life kept moving on. Everything did not stop just because we were in pain, and it even seemed like our friends at school, teachers, and neighbors just kept living their lives, too.

This was a time of self-discovery for me. I had to learn a lot of lessons about myself and my thoughts and emotions during this time. It's amazing how we can interpret things in our environment incorrectly, but we start believing them as truths. I went through a period of self-destruction as I entered the end of high school and the beginning of my college. **I had to learn about who I was, what was important to me, and what I stood for. I had to rediscover that I am loved and lovable. I had to learn about forgiveness** as my broken heart healed and I welcomed my mom back into my life.

Just a side note, my parents never got back together after many years of living in the same town. There was a day, however, when I believe there was forgiveness and maybe a healing between them. It involved a very, very long road trip to the Cleveland Airport where my mom and I were catching a flight to go see my sister in Colorado and we were riding on the bench seat in my dad's pick-up truck with me sandwiched between my mom and dad. That's another story for another day and too deeply personal to share in this book. It worked out ok in the end and maybe helped both of them move on.

So my dad somehow found a way to raise two adolescent daughters and help us get through our high school years. Well not just get through. He supported us through our sports and attended our sporting events as often as he could. He helped us with our creativity as we didn't just complete school projects but **did our very best**. He helped us deal with the highs and lows of teenage life, including dealing with friends and boyfriends and break ups from boyfriends. My dad always seemed to have the wisdom for whatever we needed. When I think of the eighties music we blared in my dad's truck while we were riding with him, I wonder what he thought about the words of the songs or our choices and influences in our lives. We did ask him later how he handled us as teens, and he keeps insisting that we "were pretty good." My sister and I see that through a slightly different lens, but that's for another story, or not.

During my childhood and teenage years before college, my dad taught my sister and me lessons in **delayed gratification**. We also learned about **saving money and even investing** in Certificates of Deposits (CDs), so the interest (which was pretty decent at that time) could **make money from your money**! He encouraged us to **plan for our future** and he demonstrated this through his own examples, such as purchasing property, building up a retirement account, investing in IRAs, securing savings bonds, and purchasing life insurance. His parents led by example and did the same before him. I was excited that I had enough money saved up to cover my first two semesters of college! Then we had to fumble through the loads of paperwork and applications and deadlines of applying for college grants and eventually student loans.

Of course we were getting into a time of our first cars. I watched my sister get her first car and I also watched all of her friends always wanting rides from her and never giving any gas money. My dad taught us about the **care and maintenance of a car** and **how to change the tires**. One lesson my dad taught us about buying things, that I have used many times in my life is, **"if someone is pushing you to buy it today or pressuring you with time before the sale runs out, be willing to walk away."** I don't know how many times this got me off of the phone with someone trying to pressure sales me. I also think of how much posture I have as I walk into car dealerships with a plan to walk out if they are not getting me what I want.

Another repeating lesson is the **power of the pause**. This is helpful in so many ways. If I find myself highly emotional, I heard it said that whatever you are going to do next, don't do it. That makes so much sense because when we react to our environment through our emotions, we could do all kinds of things we will later regret when the high emotion wears off. So **just pause…Wait!** Another way to use the pause is to **look for opportunities in storms and downturns** in the world around us or with finances. You can **look for opportunities or you can let it crush you. You can be a victim or a victor.** I'm not sure what decisions and opportunities my dad found during this chapter in his life with many storms, but I know he did as he has continued on beyond this. He has learned from mistakes. He has been willing to grow and make changes in himself. He found a way to keep living and even thriving. As a little girl, as much as I believed my dad was made of steel and that he was the strongest and wisest man in the world, I now realize that it was because he faced his challenges and fought through the storms and kept getting back up that he became stronger and wiser.

That brings me right back to my day today! It's the whole reason for my long drive and this hike! As much as I was angry and hurt and just wanted to run away, I realized that if I continue this path, I am going to go into victim mode where I hear that voice in my head say, "I can't" and then that becomes true, I can't. A lesson my dad taught through this time of facing his storms is **your energy flows where your thoughts go.** Wow! The lessons repeat at different stages and times in our lives! Today, as I wrestled with key leaders at work quitting and me being "stuck" with all of their work and mine, I was heading right into the muck of the victim mentality. With each one, I saw myself taking on one heavy load after another and carrying it until it was crushing me. No wonder I could barely get out of bed and was having such pain and tightness in my back! My brain was believing that I was really carrying weights too heavy to carry, and my back was giving out. My thoughts were on being a victim, poor me, and therefore my energy went right to that spot to support my beliefs! That spot happened to be my back. So if I take the lesson learned from my dad to **pause,** then I can begin to **look for opportunities in the**

midst of the storm. My mind will get to work finding solutions, and I will no longer have to carry the "heavy load." I can have the mindset of a winner, and my eyes can be opened to solutions all around me that I couldn't see when I was clouded with the lens of a victim. Apparently this hike and imagining the stories of the bench have taken my mind off of me and onto possibility thinking! Now I am beyond excited!

Chapter 4

There were periods of time when the bench was seemingly forgotten, and no one came around. It just sat there. The Craftsman was sad as he longed for the people to come to the bench, but he knew the very nature of people was to get busy in life, to forget to take the time to connect, to care, to love. He knew that in good times and bad, people just seem to forget. Nevertheless, the Craftsman waited by the bench, looking forward to seeing the next person who comes by, and he was willing to wait as long as it takes. While at the bench, the Craftsman inscribe a quote so all who rested there would know.

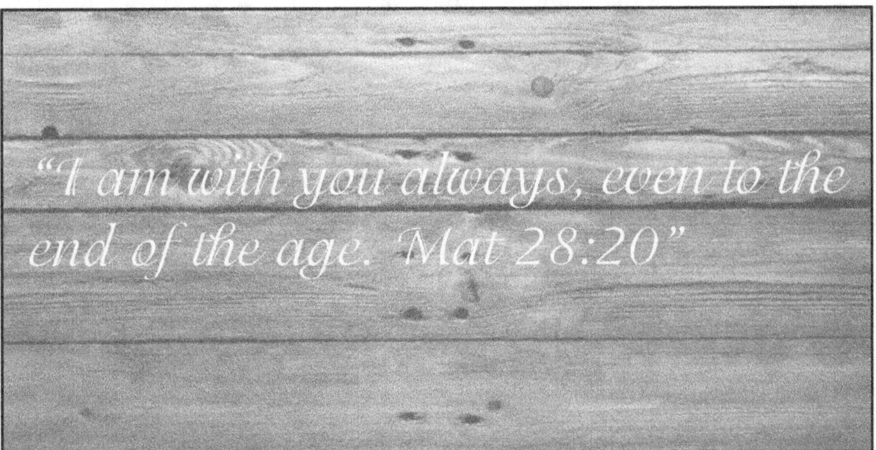

I'm not sure what the empty nest was like for my dad as my sister and I moved out of the house and went off to college. Remember, I've always seen my dad as a man of great strength who does not show much emotion, so in my imagination, he handled the empty nest just fine. I guess I never asked him.

I do remember that lingering hug my dad gave me the day I moved into my college dorm. This was a really big deal for me. Although I knew my dad loved me, hugs and big acts of affection did not happen often. I've always thought of him like the dad in the country song by Holly Dunn, "There Was Always Love In Daddy's Hands". Interestingly that song was played at my grandfather's funeral (my dad's dad) and my dad's siblings were taking about how Granddad did not express love, affection, or compliments well, but the kids knew they were loved.

I'm sure my dad's life went on just fine as my sister and I started to move on with our lives. In fact he probably continued to have many adventures of his own. Another lesson through this time was for us to stay at college rather than commute. I believe my dad was trying to teach us to **spread our wings**, to **embrace the college experience**, and to **start to gain more independence**. I went to a college that was only fifty miles from my hometown, but I stayed there and did not come home every weekend. I think that was wise of my dad to encourage this. As I had to make decisions on my own, choose the schedule of my day, and set goals on the path of my life, I remember thinking of it as a way to gain some life experience but still have the safety net under me. I knew my dad was always there, and if I had questions or if I got into a bind, he would help me out, but I also appreciated the independence.

Living in a small town, people get to know you and your regular activities. We always had pets growing up, and at some time after my sister and I went off to school, my dad got a dog. In fact he got a high energy, fun-loving, and adorable Jack Russell Terrier with a very fitting name, Zippy. My dad and his dog were inseparable. They walked a five-mile loop from where he was living at the time, along the highway to our downtown area and then back up the hill to where he lived. So many people saw my dad and his dog that they always asked me, "How's your dad and his dog?" The dog went on long and short adventures with my dad, from hikes in the woods to treasure hunts with the metal detector to fishing at the ocean.

It's interesting, when you think of the stories of the bench, how history seems to repeat itself with each new generation. My dad looked over at his daughter on the bench, holding hands with the young man, looking out over the beautiful scene. As they sat on the bench, the young man leaned over and lightly kissed her on the cheek. My dad could see by the loving way the young man looked at his daughter that soon she would be married and begin a life of their own.

My dad always treated my sister and me with utmost respect. He opened the car doors for us. He walked on the outside of the sidewalk to protect us from oncoming traffic. He did not use harsh words with us or insult us. He guided us in our dress so that we would have respect for our bodies, and if someone looked at us or talked to us in a derogatory way, he would stand up for us and protect us. My dad taught us how to be a lady by showing us how a man should treat a woman, and he taught us not to settle for anything less. He may have thought that he did not have much to offer in this area since his own marriage did not work out, but he taught us so much in how he treated us and respected us.

Some people say you marry someone who is just like your dad or mom. I did not need to marry someone like my dad, but I did need to marry someone who had what it takes to handle a woman who was shaped and developed by a father like mine…A father who loved me and respected me and taught me to learn something new every day, who taught me to **run for my dreams** and that **the big trophy is a good first goal.** A father who taught me **I can do anything I want if I work hard at it.**

My dad was always building, fixing, or inventing something. That fascination with how things work, that he had as a child, continued and really was just a way of life for him. With all those years' experience, my dad has a lot of skills and ideas to pass on. He taught my sister and me as many skills as we would show interest in, but there were still some that needed passed on. As my husband and I purchased our home and then our property and building for our business, there were lots of things that needed fixed. My dad spent time with my husband **teaching him how to weld.** This challenged my dad to go back and remember how it was to get started and some of the early skills he learned in welding, as well as the more advanced skills that made him so good at it. I held my breath at first because two of the strongest, most stubborn men I know were about to work together side by side, teacher and student, and probably have to **deal with some intensely frustrating moments** and figure out how to **keep on with the project.** As it turns out, it was a really good thing for both of them, and their relationship with each other grew. Both my husband and I are glad my dad took the time to pass on that very valuable skill.

Speaking of passing things on…When my dad retired from the JOY Mining Machinery Company, he presented me with a gift that would again influence my life in a major way. He handed me a yellow envelope, and on the outside of the envelope were the words, "Darla's Treasures". I was surprised as I opened the envelope to find all the stories and poems I had written as a young child! That was a hugely sentimental act, certainly not one I would expect from my dad who did not show emotions much! Besides being a great gift, which I was overjoyed to receive, it **confirmed the path I was taking with my life in the mental health field,** perhaps even the "calling" on my life. This gift let me see that my desire to help people was going on since I was a young child, writing stories and poems and rescuing neighbors' dogs that got loose. I was apparently noticing sad looks on people's faces since I was a little girl.

During this season of life, major events happened, such as my dad's parents passing away, first his mom, then several years later his dad. Before his dad passed, there was a time of shared caregiving where my dad spent time offering care and companionship for his dad and times I got to join them. I mentioned earlier that my dad and his siblings discussed their parents and the way they were raised, and they were surprised to see each other's views on their mom and dad's love for them and how they showed it or not. I remember my dad and I having some talks as he remembered that love was not expressed, it was assumed, and there was not a lot of place for the giving of compliments. We laughed together as I talked to my dad about how my sister and I responded to that as he raised us. We talked about how we were always trying to please him, to make him proud of us, to get that compliment. I talked to my dad about how we knew he loved us, but we felt like he never openly displayed it. It seemed like it felt safer to reveal a little more of our vulnerabilities, both mine to my dad and my dad's to me.

In the cleaning out of my grandparents' house after they passed away, my dad and I spent many hours at the house, and there were many stories of my dad growing up, the neighbors, and his siblings. We cleaned out things that were "stored for safekeeping" for generations. One of my dad's sisters wanted to make a decision about almost every item in the home, my dad wanted to get the job done. It was an interesting time, and shortly after my dad started getting rid of some of his belongings that he was holding onto. I heard him start to use the word "**simplify**." This was a lesson I did not understand the value of at that time, but later in life, it was clear to see that "stuff" in our lives can become overwhelming to us. Stuff, even good stuff, like owning cars and buildings, creates challenges of their own with taking of your time, ongoing work and maintenance, storage and expenses.

My dad had two adult daughters going their separate ways and living lives of their own, and this led to grandchildren and great-grandchildren. Now my dad was faced with the challenge of even more "lessons" to pass on to future generations and how he could somehow make their future's better.

The world feels like it is speeding up at a breakneck pace. There are changes in technology almost daily now, when before it took years before an upgrade. We have information at our fingertips. People are glued to screens almost everywhere they go, and children and infants have screens in their hands or in front of them almost as soon as they are born. Our transition from the Industrial age to the Information age is now more on the information side than the industrial side. There are major world events, such as a global pandemic, wars, political and religious division, governmental and household debt and spending that are out of control. I'm sure if I am seeing this through my eyes that it has to be amplified much larger in my dad's eyes as he looks over the years of his life and the things that have come and gone.

It's strange, in writing this chapter, the 1974 song by Harry Chapin, "Cats in the Cradle" came to my mind. I've always thought of that as such as sad song, and I still do. I've always thought that song was about someone else's life, but I realize that my life followed the same course. Good news though, it's not fate, it's not how it's supposed to be. The "Cat's In the Cradle" song represents how we live life, if we don't, on purpose, make time for each other or if we always think we have a "later" or "tomorrow." In a talk I heard by Leadership Guru and Inspirational Speaker, Dean Frey, he used the term, "Illusion of Permanence" and said it's this assumption we make that life and people in our life will just keep going on.

Perhaps through watching destruction in the lives of many people I have counseled over the years, or my dad struggle through a major surgery, or the tragic loss of a son in my life, I gained a better understanding of "urgency" of life. I don't want to look back in my life with regrets for all the could-of-been or should-have-been times to enjoy the people I love and care for. With or without the tragedies and sad stories, even if I just discovered this today, I can make "today" count and spend time with the people I love and care about… on purpose.

Chapter 5

The bench was old and rugged. Its wood was discolored, weathered, and worn. Yet there it was, sitting just a short distance off the main trail. The fall leaves were lying on its wood surface and on the ground all around the bench. The once beautiful view of the lake was beginning to grow dim as the trees and brush had grown up, showing only a hint of the beauty of the lake. The chill of the coming winter was in the air. The bench looked like something once used a long time ago but now forgotten. The Craftsman stood quietly behind the bench, filled with compassion and love for the man. It seemed as if the Craftsman was just waiting patiently for the right time to reach out and connect with the older man sitting on the bench, who was now lost in his thoughts.

An older gentleman sat quietly on the bench, holding his little dog on his lap, petting him gently. "Mon amie," he said to his dog, not just because that was the name of the dog, but he was feeling really connected to his little "friend."

The man, my dad, began reflecting on the events and memories of his life. Although he had a plan most of his adult life, he never imagined living past seventy. I have never seen my dad without a plan. His parents, one brother, a grandson, and many of his friends have passed away. He had noticed over the past several years that his body was not working like it used to. Of course there were the expected aches and pains that come from aging. No matter how healthy he had been in his forties and fifties while running all those miles of road races, choosing a healthy lifestyle in his food and nutrition, and working hard, the body just wears out. He noticed his eyes growing dim and his hands looking smaller and aged. My dad has always portrayed himself as a loner of sorts and his siblings call him a hermit. As much as he was quite comfortable being alone, many of his stories over the years have involved people, and some of the more recent involved great friends he met during his travels. When he starts planning the next trip, I always see his eyes light up with excitement as he and his friends work and plan to rendezvous in the Outer Banks of North Carolina to camp and fish and share in each other's lives. The "gang" gets together from all over, Pennsylvania, Quebec, North Carolina, and who knows where else. I have only met these friends through stories and a little over the phone, but I'm thrilled that they bring such value, energy, and friendship to my dad.

As my dad got to his late-seventies, he noticed the normal aches and pains, but he also noticed something more alarming. It seemed as though he was getting tired quicker while doing simple daily activities, like mowing the lawn or walking. The changes were not massive and could be dismissed as "normal" for someone who was seventy-seven. Fortunately though he was someone who, for years, had tracked miles and heart rates and how he was feeling during the running and hiking times, and he knew something was wrong. He was always very **observant** in all he did and was able to **use prevention instead of reaction** as a result. He talked to me about his end-of-life plans and where to find the needed documents and what action to take in the event that I got the call that something had happened to him. I always squirmed in discomfort as my Superman, my hero, the strongest man in the world, talked about a day I was not looking forward to but knew one day would happen, but not today! It was one of those necessary conversations, but nonetheless I didn't like it.

About two weeks before the scheduled stress test, my dad started to inform me of his body discomfort and about some of his concerns. He showed me that no matter how strong he is, **it's ok to ask for help**. He was taking this very seriously and started a daily text to me at 7:30 each morning. The text was simply, "all ok," to which I would respond back with my status, "all ok." I've heard it said by my friend and Inspirational speaker, Dean Frey, **"Uncertainty of your longevity creates urgency of intentionality."** Our **on-purpose daily communication** started at that time and is still going on today. At first I thought the daily texts were fun because we had never done that before, but I have grown to really appreciate them not only to know about my dad's well-being but to know that each and every day he and I are thinking about each other.

We made plans that I would give him a ride on the day of his stress test at the hospital. My dad is a great **planner** and **takes care of the details in order to keep things simple.** He also does not like to burden me as he knows I am super busy at my workplace. As a result, it felt like any other day with my dad, and in my mind, we were going to a fairly routine medical appointment. It did not take long into the appointment that the technician came to the waiting room and got me to come back with my dad as he was having the symptoms of a heart attack. Next, things sped up really fast, monitors, doctors, nurses, nitro pills, and then a trip by helicopter to Hamot Medical Center in Erie. The medical team was giving both my dad and me instructions as they were moving my dad out the door. I had the keys to his truck, and the medical team warned me not to try to beat the helicopter to Erie. That was good advice because my adrenaline was in full gear, and I would not be much support for my dad if I ended up in a wreck while going to be with him at the hospital.

The heart catheterization was complete, and my dad was in his room when I arrived at the hospital in Erie. The doctor came in shortly and talked about the blockage and the need to schedule surgery soon, maybe in a few days. Everything happened quicker than planned because overnight things worsened and there was another surgery, and before long, I was in the waiting room of the hospital while my dad was undergoing a triple bypass surgery of his heart.

I knew it was going to be a long day, so I had a couple of books I was reading and some other things to keep me occupied while I waited. My dad had a really great doctor who showed us the plans for the surgery, and I was confident that things were going to go well. Of course I prayed and I had my support team praying, too. My sister offered to come home from Colorado, but again, because I expected the best, I encouraged her not to come. I had no idea what was going to happen next, but hindsight would tell me if either of my parents were to have a major "event" in their lives like this one, I want my sister right by my side.

It truly did take all day for my dad's surgery. I was the first one in the waiting room and the last one to leave, with nearly 100 people passing through the waiting room as they waited for their loved ones. Finally I got to talk to the doctor who showed me a picture of what happened during the surgery and why it took so long. He also let me know that my dad was on the heart-lung machine for a long time, and often people take a little while longer to wake up and be able to get the breathing tube out in these situations.

They called me back into the ICU to be able to see my dad. I have never seen anyone who was in recovery from surgery that still had a breathing tube, as well as all the other medical monitors and devices still attached. I was not prepared for what I saw, and I walked into the room, looked around, started crying, and told the medical staff I would be back. I hurried out of the ICU crying my eyes out, feeling helpless and alone and wondering if I had the strength to do this. I immediately called my husband for support. He comforted me over the phone and offered me encouragement and prayer. He could not be with me because he had come down with pink eye right before we went to the hospital. I got myself back together again, took a deep breath, and went back into the ICU. This time I knew what I was going to see, I was resolved to be strong and help wherever I could, and I was no longer alone.

One day turned into two and then three, and it just went on and on. My co-workers and my mom came to the downstairs lobby area and provided me with much needed, support, and encouragement. They had to bring a little work as they brought up the paychecks so I could sign them. I barely thought about work while I was at the hospital with my dad. I stayed in a hotel some days and went home on others. There were times of great progress and times of great setbacks. My own self-care was greatly deprived, and it wasn't until my dad finally got out of the hospital that I realized that I had not been outside in the sun, or outside at all, for most of the time he was in the hospital. We made it through. My dad stayed with my husband and me for about a month after his surgery. It turns out that the surgery went great, and my dad's healing was moving on ahead of its target. The nurses that came to the house were impressed with his progress. My dad and I started walking short walks together with his dog. These were nice. My dad was healing so well, I saw so much life and energy in him. He continued to be super cautious just to make sure all was ok. The follow up appointment with the cardiologist proved that all was truly ok. We asked the doctor what limitations or restrictions my dad has. The doctor pretty much advised my dad not to jump out of an airplane, but other than that, he can do just about anything he wants. I heard that loud and clear, Superman was back!

After my dad went back to his own home, we continue to walk together every Wednesday morning, and we still do that today. I let my employees at work know that on Wednesdays from 8 A.M. to 9 A.M., I will be walking with my dad and I do not want any interruptions with calls or texts unless it is life or death. This is my time with my dad, and it is sacred. We talk about everything during our walks, and sometimes we just enjoy the silence.

Now eighty-one-years-old, he sighed and thought to himself, "I'm just tired." He thought of his daughters who struggled to talk with him about his aging process and the reality that one day he would not be here. After all these years, he was still true to his word to continue teaching his daughters something new. This time it was about the **lesson of facing the tough stuff, like talking about the end of life and the aging process,** even though I always thought he was an emotion avoider.

As he sat on the bench, he pondered his faith, which had always been very private for him but important nonetheless. It seemed like in nature, he could find closeness or connection to his Lord. It reminded him of some of his religious upbringing like in the 23rd Psalm, "The Lord is my shepherd…He leads me beside the still waters…"

His thoughts were interrupted as his daughter arrived with hurried steps and a big smile. This was the day they were going to walk together and just spend some time with each other. The daughter always referred to this time as "Dad time." It was always exciting to connect with each other, laugh at the crazy world we live in, sort through struggles of the day, or just enjoy nature together. She loved spending time with him and being able to talk about anything and everything. Her dad has always offered so much wisdom and was so well-read and interested that he could talk about just about anything.

Today she seemed different, full of energy, almost giddy, like she was up to something. She was carrying an interesting item, which reminded him of something old, yet it had something mysterious about it like a treasure. She handed it over to her dad without saying a word at first, just smiling. He looked at her with a raised eyebrow as he does not like surprises. Finally she said, "I made you something. I know you are getting ready to leave for North Carolina and I hope that one of the days during your trip, when you are at the beach or at your campsite, you will open this and enjoy it."

They stood and got ready for their walk. Earlier, when he sat down on the bench today, he was so caught up in his own thoughts that he did not notice the inscription on the bench, but now as he stood to his feet, he saw it...

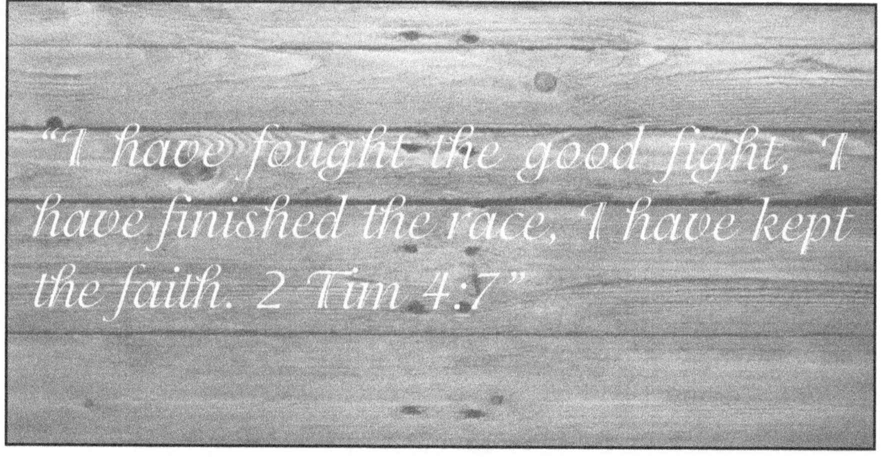

And the Craftsman of the bench saw him see it, and he smiled. Then the Craftsman reached over the bench and whispered into the man's ears, "Well done, my good and faithful servant" Mat 25:21.

Although this final chapter is the end of the book, it is the place where the story began. It was the time I learned that my dad was struggling with being tired, unsure why he was still here, and wondering if he had made a difference. I did not set out to write a book, but I did intend on letting my dad know what an incredible impact he made on my life. Words sometimes get awkward when we just try to speak them, so maybe the message just needs to be seen or experienced.

Conclusion

You see, benches really cannot tell stories, but in every human life, there is a story to tell. Some people never get a chance to spend time with a person or connect with them in a way that a piece of their story is heard. Some people never get to know that the way they interacted with the world impacted it and made a difference, even if to just one person. This impact is the thing they are going to leave behind. This is their legacy. We know from experience that when we touch one person's life, there is usually a chain reaction from this one impact that ripples on to person after person after that. It is unknown how many lives we impact positively as we look at someone and smile, or do a random act of kindness for them, or if we sit on the bench with them, look out at the beautiful view, and just be present with them, listening as they tell their story.

This is just one of the stories of the bench. It seems as if the Craftsman created the bench in such a clever way to draw people to it, to each other, and to Him through the beauty of His creation and the incredible way we can enjoy it through all our senses and hold those experiences deep in our hearts and minds.

This story of the bench is the story of the lessons I learned from my dad, one of the greatest heroes in my life, and the amazing legacy he will leave behind. When I started with my dad's commitment to bring children into the world and teach them one new thing every day, I laughed out loud as I started to calculate how many days I have been alive. I imagined being annoying and listing all of the lessons learned, but fortunately for you, the reader, and for my dad, I did not do that. Let's see, at the time of writing this book, I am fifty-one years, three months, and fifteen-days-old. Converted to days, I have been on this earth for 18,720 days. Even if my dad intended to teach my sister and me one new thing every day from birth to age eighteen, that is still a commitment of 6,570 new things. I'd say he hit that one way out of the park!

This book is simply a story of some of the lessons I learned from him, and the book is for him as a message of a daughter's love for her father. This is not intended to be the complete story of my dad's life, in fact this story involves a lot of imagination for the times of his life that I really don't have the information, or maybe just a story or two about my dad as told by my grandparents or my aunts and uncles, or something I saw through our home movies when my sister and I were babies. Then, as the story continues, I have more direct knowledge and memories because I was born and living at the time and actually interacting with my dad. Even then my view might be distorted because I see things through my eyes and my interpretation and my limited life experience. That makes me wonder as a parent which lessons my daughter may have "picked up" or "caught" from me that might be a little distorted by not having the whole story. I can only hope that if she received lessons from my mistakes or strengths as a parent that she can ask me the questions and learn the true lesson intended.

If this book was intended to be a story of my dad's life, I would need years to write it because he lived in a way that is far more dynamic and expansive than I could put in this book. His adventures alone could fill a book as lengthy as J. R. R. Tolkien's *The Hobbit*. There would be stories in his book about working hard, overcoming obstacles, going on adventures, hiking parts of the Appalachian Trail, teaching, and investing in young people wherever he goes, finding treasure in people and finding treasure in the ground, and of course there is likely to be a fish story or two. There would be friends from work, big game hunting out west, helping neighbors and strangers, computer clubs, and fishing tournaments. I'm sure there would be stories about the Iditarod Sled Dog Race in Alaska and trips to Colorado. There would be a friend from Quebec and other friends from North Carolina. There would be stories about the guy in the bait shop or someone at the ferry terminal.

Like I said, that was not the intention of this book. The intention was simply to answer my dad's question, did I make a difference? Did my life matter? I wanted him to know the answer for sure, even though I believe he already knows, and I wanted him to know the message of this book when he is still alive. We don't know if we have tomorrow. None of us do.

One man who lived life to the best he knew how, learning new things, investing in himself and others…One man who saw himself as a people avoider, who invested into the lives of his two daughters and taught daily lessons as he committed to do when he decided to have children. The daughters have grown and are passing the life lessons to their children and grandchildren, and through their work and ministry, the daughters are carrying on the legacy of their dad and touching lives all over the world. The impact of one man, and the seeds early planted, can change the world in ways we could never imagine.

How many people, our moms, dads, sisters, brothers, friends, and loved ones, get to the final chapters of their lives not knowing if they've made a difference or if their lives even mattered? How many times are there grudges or anger or fear that we have held onto for years that is stopping us from connecting to others and allowing our lives to intersect? What if we could solve one of the mysteries that the Craftsman left for us and realize that it's all about relationships? Maybe then we would set aside our differences, sit down on the bench together, look out over the beautiful landscape, and just listen to each other's story. Imagine the impact…

Afterword

I have the utmost love and respect for my dad. He is a very private person. In the writing of this book, I constantly checked myself to see if the book or any part of the book would dishonor or offend my dad in any way. In light of him being a private person, I am making a commitment to my dad that his book is the <u>only</u> book, unless he were to give me permission to share it with others or even set out to get it published.

In the very writing of this book, it is amazing to me how I continue to learn new things and how the old lessons my dad has taught me come to life in new ways in different stages of my life. The writing of this book not only taught me new things, but it has given me an even closer connection to my dad and it has been transforming and renewing for me.

As I was writing this book, just like any author, there were times that I was stuck and couldn't seem to move the book forward. I'd have to analyze what was going on, so I could identify the barrier and then remove it or work through it. One of those times was just a change that was needed in the order of things. As I was studying my storyboard, it popped out at me, and once again the writing continued. Then shortly after that, I got to the place where my head was telling me to finish the book, but there was something stopping me, creating an incredible anxiety, and causing me to avoid writing. Every time I thought about writing the book, I was overcome with anxiety and I avoided it. I asked myself "why" and I was unable to come up with anything rational that would stop me from writing the book. I even asked myself, "Are you afraid to finish the book because somehow that will show you are 'ready' to face it when your dad passes away and that somehow it will make it 'ok' if he dies?" I knew that was absurd, but still the anxiety persisted.

I was talking with my husband and I asked him to coach me to see if we could discover what was holding me back. After talking for awhile and answering some questions, he asked me to write down on a notecard my "why" for writing the book, and was this still true today like it was when I decided to begin writing? I quickly began writing. The reason why I am writing this book is to show my dad how much he has impacted my life and that his life did indeed matter, not just to me but in the ripple effect that it has caused to all he has touched and all my sister and I have touched as a result of the life lessons he taught to us. I also said another reason I have to get the book done is because I want to tell my dad while he is still alive and not just make a tribute to him after he has passed away. I thought of all the ways to express this to my dad and I felt like the greatest way to show my love and appreciation was to write it down, so he can read it instead of me stumbling with my words and emotions when I try to say it.

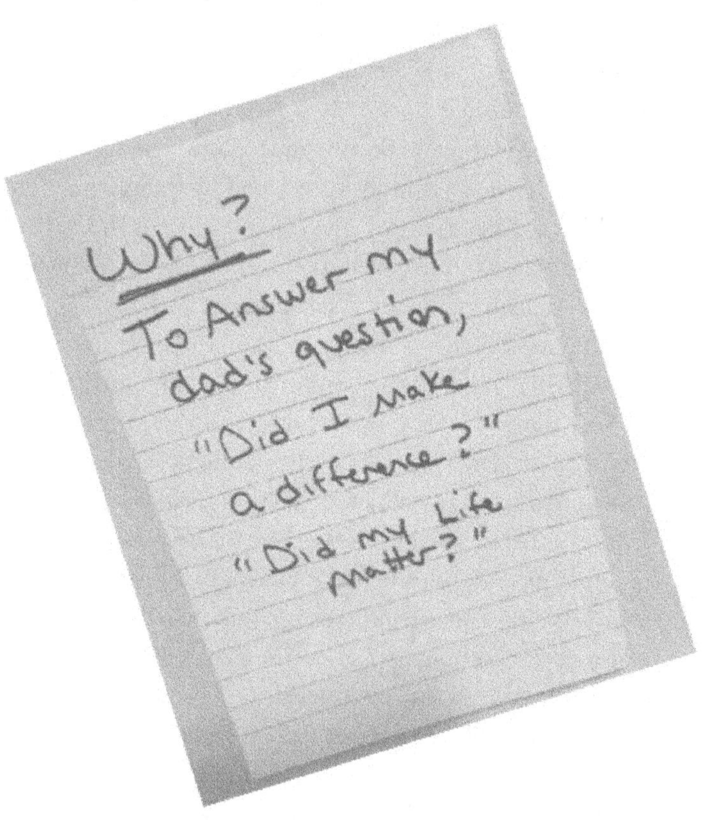

As my husband and I were talking and I was reading my "why" back to him, I was filled with an overwhelming sense of anxiety. I noticed it and realized it is the same feeling I feel when I sit down to write. I focused on the anxiety to try to understand the source.

I told my husband that my dad is such a private person and he does not like intense emotions, so I am terrified to finish the book and give it to my dad because I am afraid that my dad will become upset with me and I'm so afraid to lose the relationship I have with him. As we discovered where this irrational fear came from, I knew it was more important to share my message of love to my dad through the book than to avoid the emotional challenges that presenting the book to my dad might bring.

Interesting, remember the black book of lies I mentioned when our cat got into the butter? Well that same fear of being "cast out of the family" is like this fear that I am describing today. It did not take me long to realize that my little girl fear of being cast out of my family was so far from the truth, but it felt true to me back then, and I must have carried that with me into my adult years. Amazing, a fear of doing something that might be unpleasant brought up a memory from the past where once again I misinterpreted my environment and family, and now the lesson is being learned, even as I am writing this book!

There were countless other lessons in the writing of this book that were borrowed from my growing up days with my dad. As in the example above, I learned about overcoming fears and struggles by challenging things we believed from the past, things that held us captive and prevented us from being all we can be. I had to remember how to overcome roadblocks and use creative problem-solving. I had to remember how to stay focused on the goal so you can keep on going, even when you don't feel like it. In the writing of the book, my Wednesday walks with my dad continued, so I was able to see the wisdom of my dad more clearly and experience his connection and love for me.

That one day that I was struggling, when I first encountered the bench and this story started coming alive, I had an amazing victory that day, which was not realized until I continued writing the story. I was struggling with problems at work and I did not know how to solve them. I was feeling inadequate and alone, and my negative thoughts that flooded my mind confirmed that to me over and over. As I began developing the story of the bench, I was reminded of the lessons of the past. Then I made the discovery: I already had what I needed from my previous lessons. I was able to glean from my dad's wisdom, and he could continue to guide, me even when he is not present. VIC-TORY! The victory is this discovery!

Lessons in life are not one and done, but like a good book, you can read it at different times in your life and get a new lesson or a new understanding of your current situation. I was surprised to hear from my children when they graduated from high school that they thought they should "know" what to do and that someone should have "taught" them this or that. Someone once told me that your learning just begins when you get out of high school. I say it begins when we are babies (or possibly in the womb) and it continues our whole life, right up until the day we die. There is freedom in that because we don't have to have all the answers, we just have to be willing to learn.

As much as I have wanted the writing of The Bench to be a love letter to my dad, I am starting to see that the book is as much for me as it is for him. In the time of the writing of this book, I was in a time of my life with daily struggles. Struggles to get out of bed in the morning and a lack of motivation. Struggles with my own negative thoughts, which I carried throughout my days. Struggles with people and possibly burnout. I certainly had lost my zest somewhere along the way.

So with the lesson, "tell the truth" and "do not tell a lie" and all the other character lessons, I did not want to pour all my misery and negativity onto my dad when we talked or when I answered his text with "all ok." At 7:30 every morning, I receive a text from my dad that simply says "all ok." He has been doing this every day since the heart surgery. I respond back "all ok" to confirm my own well-being and the receipt of his text. So when I get the text and I am not feeling ok, mostly because of my stinking thinking, I cannot lie. I have to give myself a pep talk and get my mind in the right place by changing my focus to the positive for the day in order for me to be honest when I reply "all ok." I do give my dad a lot of credit. Who would have thought that a simple morning text would help shape each day by getting my thoughts in the right place? I'd say this is a multiplication effect of the lessons caught and taught and one that affects me and everyone I interact with.

The impact of reviewing the lessons learned and the stories of the bench have helped bring me back to life and remember who I am. I have a stronger connection with my dad, sister, and mom. I have learned to love deeply and value relationships and get back to humanity with compassion and love, which have gotten lost somewhere along the way. Perhaps I got too busy with life and forgot to spend time on the bench with the people around me…

I know my dad is brilliant, but there was no way he could have known that his promise to teach his children one new thing every day would continue whether or not he was there to do the teaching! I do know that our Father, in Heaven, does know us that well, and from knitting us together in our mother's womb to walking with us through the valley of the shadow of death, He is with us, and all of the connections and relationships in our lives continue to impact each other and all those around us.

Letter to my dad:

One day, Dad, I will have to say my final good bye to you here on this earth. There is nothing that I will enjoy about that day because of course I want to keep you in my life forever. I know I have what it takes to make it through that sad time and that I carry all the lessons I need to continue on with my life and dreams. I will always carry you with me as I hear your voice when I walk in the woods, or when I sit on the bench and ponder the struggles or worries of the day. Thank you, Dad, for all of you that you have poured into me, making me to be the person that I am today. I will carry on your legacy and make one of my own. I will keep living and striving and dreaming until that day that I get to join you in Heaven with our Lord and Savior. I love you, Dad!

"*Carry your pain into a new chapter and choose to keep living.*"

Dean Frey

"The discovery
of the bench …"